Disgusting Jokes

for kids

First published in Great Britain 1988 by Ward Lock Limited,
8 Clifford Street, London W1X 1RB, an Egmont company.

This edition published 2004 by Bounty Books,
a division of Octopus Publishing Group Ltd,
2-4 Heron Quays, London E14 4JP
Reprinted 2004, 2005, (Twice), 2008
ISBN 978-0-753708-79-8

Printed and bound in Dubai

Disgusting Jokes

for kids

Bounty
Books

If cows could fly,
what might you get?
A pat on the head.

CH LA LA!!!

Customer: 'Do you have pigs' feet?'
Butcher: 'Yes, madam.'
Customer: 'Well, wear proper shoes and no one will notice.'

Doctor: 'Come over to the window, Mr. Ample, and stick out your tongue.'
Mr. Ample: 'Why, do you want a better look, doctor?'
Doctor: 'No, I want to pay my neighbours back for their son's rudeness.'

Doctor, doctor, I've got a pain in my lower back!
    We must get to the bottom of this!
What do you get if you cross a parrot with a centipede?
    A walkie talkie.

What's the difference between a coyote and a flea?
    One howls on a prairie, the other prowls on the hairy!

What's the difference between a toilet brush and a biscuit?
    You can't dip a toilet brush in your tea!

What did the leopard say when he ate the explorer?
    Mmm, that hit the spot.

COFF! COFF! COFF!

Why do undertakers often catch colds?
   Because they're always surrounded by coffin.

What happened when a skunk did a bank robbery?
   The police were soon on the scent.

How do you turn ants into underwear?
   Put a 'P' in front of them.

What kind of tree can't you climb?
   A lavatory.

What's the smelliest game you can play?
Ping-Pong!

What do you call a skeleton that refuses to dance?
Lazy bones.

What's white outside, black inside and wriggles about?
A cockroach sandwich.

Waiter, waiter, there's a button in my stew.
     I expect it fell off the jacket potato, sir.

Why did Smart Alec's sense of touch suffer when he wasn't well?
     Because he didn't feel well.

What was the fly doing in the alphabet soup?
     Learning to spell.

Barry: 'Is your sister pretty or is she ugly?'
Harry: 'Well, I'd say she was pretty ugly.'

Doctor, will I lose my looks as I get older?
     With any luck, yes!

If your nose runs and your feet smell, are you built upside-down?

Doctor, doctor, how can I stop my nose running?
Stick out your foot and trip it up.

Ben: 'Is your mother a good cook?'
Tim: 'Not really. In fact our dustbin is the only one in the street that gets indigestion.'

Why did Smart Alec take his nose apart?
    To see how it ran!

City Sid: 'Do these cows really give milk?'
Farmer Fred: 'Well, they don't exactly give it.
You have to squeeze it out of them.'

Did you hear about the farmer who had such long
toenails he used them to plough a field?

Doctor, doctor! I keep thinking I'm a piece of rope!
    Get knotted!

Why didn't Smart Alec's sister get a job as a milkmaid?
    Because she couldn't tell one end of the cow from the udder!

What happens when a witch loses her temper?
    She flies off the handle.

Dora: 'Do you like my new hairstyle?'
Thora: 'Well, it helps to cover up your face!'

Selma: 'I've ordered twenty pints of milk so I can bath like Cleopatra.'
Thelma: 'Pasteurised?'
Selma: 'I'd be happy if it comes up to my waist.'

Why was the skeleton miserable at the party?
  Because he had no body to dance with.

What did one vulture say to the other?
  I've a bone to pick with you.

Did you hear about the man who went to the doctor and asked for something for his liver? He came home with a pound of onions!

Why were the skeleton's teeth chattering?
    Because he was chilled to the marrow.

Old gentleman: 'My barber gives me what I call a "road map" shave.'
Hairdresser: 'What's that?'
Old gentleman: 'He leaves my face full of short cuts!'

What happened when someone kicked the skeleton on both shins?
    He hadn't a leg to stand on.

What kind of ice do vampires like?
  Ice-scream!

Teacher: 'There's a saying that an apple a day keeps the doctor away.'
Smart Alec: 'It does if you throw it hard enough.'

What did the monster say to the grand piano?
  What beautiful teeth you've got.

What entertainment do ghosts attend at Christmas?
    Phantomimes.

Mr. Brown: 'Did you put Mum's cake out for the birds?'
Tommy: 'Yes.'
Mr. Brown: 'You naughty boy. Why should they suffer too!'

What do short-sighted ghosts wear?
    Spooktacles!

A vampire was giving a party. The invitations read: Fancy a bite? Come round Saturday night!

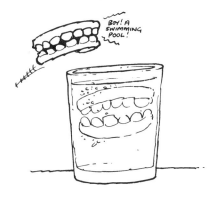

'Your teeth are like stars', he said,
Pressing her hand so white.
He spoke the truth, for like the stars,
Her teeth came out at night!

What did the strict father ghost say to his son?
     Spook only when you are spooken to.

*What runs around all day and lies down at night
with its tongue hanging out?*
     A training shoe.

Peter: 'I'm so thirsty my tongue's hanging out.'
Paul: 'Is that horrible spotted thing your tongue? I thought it was your tie!'

Hotel Guest: 'Are the sheets in the hotel clean?'
Manager: 'Certainly, sir. They were washed yesterday. If you don't believe me, feel them. They're still damp.'

Allie: 'Will you join me in a cup of tea?'
Sally: 'Do you think there'd be enough room for the two of us?'

Samantha: 'I'm no fool.'
Smart Alec: 'Your opinion doesn't count against one hundred others.'

Smart Alec: 'Don't look out of the window.'
Dennis: 'Why not?'
Smart Alec: 'People will think it's Halloween!'

Margaret: 'Whenever I'm down in the dumps I buy myself a new pair of shoes.'
Melissa: 'So that's where you get them!'

Why don't centipedes play football?
Because by the time they've got their boots on, it's time to go home.

What time is it when you have to go to the dentist?
Two thirty!

What does a ghost keep in his cellar?
  Whines and spirits!

What creature can eat faster than any other?
  A goblin.

What happens to wasps that are sick?
  They're taken to waspital.

Sheila: 'I just came back from the beauty salon.'
Smart Alec: 'Pity it was closed!'

Why do giraffes have long necks?
    Because their feet smell really bad.

What do you give a pig with spots?
    Oinkment!

OH YEAH!

What do you give a seasick elephant?
    An awful lot of room.

What's black and white, black and white, black and white?
    A penguin rolling down a hill.

Sally: 'My doctor's just put me on the olive oil diet.'
Allie: 'Have you lost weight?'
Sally: 'No, but I've stopped squeaking!'

Did you hear about the village idiot buying bird seed? He said he wanted to grow some birds!

What's yellow and extremely stupid?
   Thick custard.

Smart Alec: 'Is your new girlfriend pretty?'
Dennis: 'I'll say. She has long blonde hair all down her back.'
Smart Alec: 'Pity it's not on her head!'

Keith: 'Do you hold your girlfriend's hand?'
Kevin: 'Yes, but I wish the rest of her would come round and see me more often.'

Why couldn't Dracula's wife get to sleep?
Because she was kept awake by her husband's coffin.

What does a fiend do on Saturday night?
He takes his girl fiend out.

Smart Alec: What's your new head teacher like?'
Andrew: 'Not too bad. He grows on you.'
Smart Alec: 'You mean he's like a wart.'

Waiter, waiter, you've got your thumb in my soup!
    It's alright sir, it isn't hot.

Why is the sausage the rudest food?
    Because it spits.

Waiter, waiter, is this cottage pie?
    Yes, sir.
Well fetch a doctor. I think I've just swallowed a window pane.

Waiter, waiter, this lobster's only got one claw!
    It must have been in a fight, sir.
Then bring me the winner.

What happened when Smart Alec dreamed he was eating his pillow?
    He woke up feeling down in the mouth.

Which team plays cricket when half undressed?
    The Vest Undies.

Mrs. Brown: 'Did you wash that fish before you cooked it?'
Mr. Brown: 'What's the point in washing something that has spent all its life in water?'

Waiter, this coffee tastes like dishwater!
How do you know that, sir?

Waiter, waiter, there's a fly in my chicken soup!
It's the bad meat that attracts them, sir!

What do you call a reptile that suffers from seasickness?

An illigator.

How do you make a loo roll?

Throw it down a hill.

Why was the man arrested for looking at sets of dentures in the dentist's window?

Because it was against the law to pick your teeth in public.

Why did Dim Dinah fall out the window?
　　Because her mum asked her to iron the curtains!

What did the mayonnaise say to the fridge?
　　Close the door, I'm dressing!

Why did the tomato blush?
　　Because it saw the lettuce undressed.

Mum: 'Did you have a nice meal with Tommy and Mrs. Atkinson?'
Smart Alec: 'It was out of this world.'
Mum: 'Really, it was that good?'
Smart Alec: 'No. But it was full of Unidentified Frying Objects!'

Who wrote How To Make A Million?
   Robin Banks.

Did you know that only dirty people need
to wash?

A TRAMP!
I LIKE TRAMP!

What happened when the monster lost a hand?
   He went to a second-hand shop.

Why did the businessman live without a bathroom?
   Because he was filthy rich.

Did you hear about the man who read the obituary columns and thought it strange that people died in alphabetical order?

How do you flatten a ghost?
    With a spirit level.

What kind of mistakes are ghosts likely to make?
    Boo-boos!

Knock! Knock!
    Who's there?
Blue.
    Blue who?
Oh, do stop crying!

Baby bear: 'Who's been eating my porridge?'
Mummy bear: 'Who's been eating my porridge?'
Daddy bear: 'Buuurrrppp!'

Doctor, doctor, that ointment you gave me made my leg smart.
Try rubbing some on your head then.

Doctor: 'You look very flushed, Mrs. Perkins. You must have flu.'
Mrs. Perkins: 'No, doctor. I came on the bus.'

Mr. Thick: 'When I was young we were so poor we only ate once a day.'
Mr. Thin: 'So what! We were so poor we only had one measle at a time.'

Freddie: 'Ugh! I just ate a strawberry with a maggot in it.'
Faye: 'Have some water to wash it down.'
Freddie: 'No, let it walk.'

Where did the funny ghost get his jokes?
   From a crypt writer!

Sally: 'I have a hunch.'
Smart Alec: 'Oh, I just thought you were round shouldered.'

Milly: 'My boyfriend says I'm beautiful.'
Molly: 'That's 'cos love is blind.'

Do you always bathe in dirty water?
   It wasn't dirty before I got in.

Annie: 'Where do you bathe when you go camping?'
Danny: 'In the spring.'
Annie: 'I said where, not when!'

Gillie: 'How did Mum know you hadn't had a wash?'
Willie: 'I forgot to dirty the towel.'

Smart Alec: 'What's your perfume called?'
Sally: 'High Heaven.'
Smart Alec: 'Mmm, it certainly stinks to it!'

What do you get if you cross a skunk with a boomerang?
    A smell you can't get rid of!

What's a vampire's favourite dance?
    The last vaults.

I DON'T UNDERSTAND THAT JOKE!

*What do you get if you cross a skunk with
a wasp?*
  Something that stinks and stings.

What is a baby skunk's ambition?
  To make a big stink.

Did you hear about the short-sighted skunk that
fell in love with the sewage pipe?

What did the skunk say when the wind changed?
  It's all coming back to me now!

Why did the whale blush?
  Because the seaweed.

What do you call a baby whale that cries a lot?
    A little blubber.

What has antlers and sucks your blood?
    A moose-quito.

What's the difference between a flea and a cat?
    A cat can have fleas but a flea can't have cats.

What did the dog say to the flea?
    Stop bugging me.

What did the dog say when it sat on sandpaper?
    Rough!

Why were the elephants arrested when they went swimming?
    They couldn't keep their trunks up.

What monster can sit on the end of your finger?
   A bogeyman.

What happens if you get a stomach upset on December 24th?
   Christmas 'eave!

Sam: 'Did you miss me when I went away?'
Sue: 'Did you go away?'

Mandy: 'Will you still love me when I'm old and grey?'
Mike: 'I do, don't I!'

Mr. Pigsfeet: 'Is that steak and kidney pie I smell?'
Mrs. Pigsfeet: 'It is, and you do.'

Host at party: 'And is this your most charming husband?'
Mrs. Brown: 'No, but he's the only one I've got.'

Is it polite to eat sausages with your fingers?
No, fingers should be eaten separately.

What do you call a monster with a sausage on its head?
A head-banger.

Why did Frankenstein go to evening classes?
   Because they had a body-building session.

What do you call a beautiful, polite monster?
   A failure.

What do sea monsters eat?
   Fish and ships.

What did the policeman say to the three-headed monster?
   Hello, hello, hello.

Smart Alec's brother has a leaning towards pretty girls.

Yes, but they push him back!

Mother: 'Alec! Wash your face. I can see what you had for breakfast!'
Smart Alec: 'What did I have?'
Mother: 'Fried eggs.'
Smart Alec: 'Wrong, that was yesterday!'

And does Eric like being a chimney sweep?

Yes, it really soots him.

Mr. Grumble: 'This stew's half cold.'
Mrs. Grumble: 'Well eat the half that's hot.'

Clive: 'Do you think I'm handsome?'
Claire: 'Mmm, in a way.'
Clive: 'What way?'
Claire: 'As far away as possible!'

Waiter: 'And how did you find your pork chop, sir?'
Diner: 'Oh, I just moved a pea and there it was.'

What did the cannibal say to the cook when he caught a monk?
　　You can't stew him, he's a friar.

HEAVENS – WHAT AN AWFUL JOKE!

Mr. Smith: 'I hate paying my gas bill.'
Mr. Jones: 'You should pay all your bills with a smile.'
Mr. Smith: 'I've tried that, but they still insist on money.'

What did the ghost play on the piano?
   A haunting tune.

What did Dim Dennis do with the toothpaste?
   Tried to stick his loose tooth back in.

Sam: 'Does your mum make good toast?'
Shane: 'That's a burning question!'

Darren: 'I'm not good looking, and I don't have an expensive car or a racing yacht like Danny, but I really love you.'
Daisy: 'I love you too, but tell me more about Danny.'

Householder: 'I'll teach you to throw stones at my window!'
Cheeky Charlie: 'I wish you would, I keep missing.'

Why is a small boy like a woolly jumper?
    They both shrink from washing.

Milly: 'Why do they call your brother the space cadet?'
Molly: 'Because he's got so much space between his ears.'

Mr. Brown: 'I'm home dear, you can serve the salad.'
Mrs. Brown: 'How did you know we were having salad?'
Mr. Brown: 'I couldn't smell anything burning.'

Doctor, doctor, I feel like a sheep!
    That's too baaaaad!

What do you call a woman who slides about on bread?
    Marge.

Little Mary had a cow,
She fed it safety pins.
And every time she milked that cow,
The milk came out in tins.

Doctor, doctor, I feel like a pair of curtains!
    Pull yourself together, man!

Doctor, doctor, I've only got 50 seconds to live.
    Just sit over there a minute.

Doctor, doctor, I feel like a yo-yo.
    Sit down, stand up, sit down, stand up...

Doctor, doctor, can you cure my pimples?
    I never make rash promises!

Doctor, doctor I think I'm a budgie.
    I'll tweet you in a minute.

What did the beaver say to the tree?
    It sure is good to gnaw you.

Doctor: 'And did you drink your medicine after your bath?'
Mrs. Soap: 'No, doctor. By the time I'd drunk the bath there wasn't enough room for the medicine.'

What does a vampire doctor say?
   Necks, please!

What travels through the water at 100 mph, eating everything in sight?
   A motor pike.

What's green and covered in red spots?
    A frog with measles.

Teacher: 'Give me a sentence using the word 'urchin'.'
Lucy: 'Urchin was so pointed it it almost met 'er nose.'

Teacher: 'Harry, have you ever had your eyes checked?'
Harry: 'No, miss, they've always been green.'

Ted: 'How's your nose?'
Fred: 'Shut up!'
Ted: 'So is mine. Must be the weather.'

When are eyes not eyes?
    When cold winds make them water.

What's a skeleton's favourite vegetable?
    Marrow.

What do you call a steam-roller that runs over a skeleton?
    A bone-crusher.

What do you call a man who's been buried for thousands of years?
   Pete.

What did the zombie say when he entered the morgue?
   Anybody home?

What's a ghost's favourite Italian food?
   Spookhetti.

What's the devil's favourite drink?
   Demonade.

Do undertakers enjoy their job?
    Of corpse they do!

What did Dracula receive after the first film they made about him?
    Fang mail.

How do you join Dracula's fan cub?
    You send your name, your address and your blood group.

Why are demons and ghouls so happy together?
Because a demon is a ghoul's best friend.

Who was known as the Chiropodist King?
William the Corncurer.

Why did Smart Alec's eccentric uncle hide under the bed?
Because he thought he was a little potty.

Why does a tap drip?
Because it doesn't have a handkerchief.

What did Eric win when he lost four stone in weight?
The No-Belly Prize!

Waiter, waiter, there's a hair in this pie!
Well, you did ask for rabbit pie, sir.

What did one skeleton say to the other?
If we had any guts we'd get out of here!

What do you call a nervous sorcerer?
  A twitch.

Where do you find ghost snails?
  At the end of ghost's toes.

Knock! Knock!
  Who's there?
Armageddon.
  Armageddon who?
Armageddon out of here!

Why was Frankenstein's monster fond of Frankenstein?

Because he kept him in stitches.

Why are mummies good at keeping secrets?

Because they keep things under wraps.

Why did the mummy leave its tomb after 2000 years?

It thought it was old enough to leave home.

Doctor, doctor, I feel like a piano.

Hang on while I make some notes.

What do you call a baby witch?
    A Hallowe'eny!

What kind of shoe does a witch wear in summer?
    Open-toad sandals.

How does a witch tell the time?
    By her witch-watch.

First skeleton: 'Brr, it's cold today'.
Second skeleton: 'Yes, that wind's blowing right through me.'

Mummy, Mummy, why can't we have a dustbin like everybody else?

Just stop talking and start chewing!

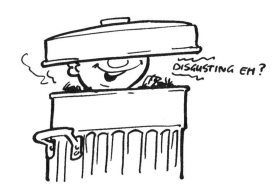

DISGUSTING EH?

Whom does a monster ask for a date?

Any old ghoul he can find!

When two friends stick together, is it because they don't wash often enough?

What does a modern witch ride?
   A broom-broomstick.

Mum: 'What would you say if I sat down at the table with hands as filthy as yours?'
Smart Alec: 'I'd be too polite to mention it.'

Waiter, waiter, why is my apple pie all squashed?
   You did ask me to step on it, sir.

Sarah: 'Did you hear about Trisha?'
Sandra: 'Who's she?'
Sarah: 'She's that optician's daughter who keeps making a spectacle of herself.'

Doctor, doctor, those pills you gave me to make me stronger aren't doing any good at all.

How can you tell?

I can't unscrew the bottle!

What's the difference between a bus driver and a cold in the head?

A bus driver knows when to stop, and a cold in the head stops the nose!

Waiter, waiter, there's a hand in my soup!
    That's not your soup dish, sir, that's the finger bowl!

Sally: 'Our teacher has what's called a sympathetic face.'
Wally: 'What do you mean?'
Sally : 'People look at him and feel sympathetic.'

How can you make a snail move faster?
    Take away its food.

Kevin: 'I'm a liar, you know.'
Keith: 'I don't believe you.'

Doctor, doctor, it's wonderful! I feel like my old self again!
In that case we'd better start a new course of treatment.

Alan: 'Please, miss, can I leave the room?'
Teacher: 'Well you can't take it with you.'

What smells worse than Alec's feet?
Alec's feet and Andrew's feet.

What's a cheerful flea called?
  A hoptimist.

What does a deaf fisherman need?
  A herring aid.

How can a flea be a space invader?
  When it takes up residence in an idiot's ear.

What's a vampire's favourite fruit?
  A blood orange.

I PREFER
SEEDLESS GRAPES
ACTUALLY

What brings a monster's babies?
Frankenstork.

Why are vampire families so close?
Because blood is thicker than water.

Teacher: 'What's the difference between the death rate in the Middle Ages and today?'
Smart Alec: 'The same – one per person.'

YE
DEADE
BODDE

Paul: 'Could you be happy with a boy like me?'
Pam: 'Well, as long as he wasn't too much like you.'

What do you get if you cross an elephant with an expensive carpet?
 A thick pile.

What does an executioner do with a piece of paper and a pencil?
 Writes his chopping list.

Mrs. Jones: 'Our baby's such a happy little girl. She has such an infectious smile.'
Mrs. Smith: 'Then tell her not to smile near me.'

New customer: 'Your hands don't look clean.'
Hairdresser: 'No, I haven't done a shampoo all morning.'

Andy: 'Your dad is a man of many parts.'
Smart Alec: 'Yes, but I don't think they put him together very well.'

Catch a vampire before it catches ... aarrgghh!

What did one magician say to another?
    Who was that girl I sawed you with last night?

She can't see beyond the end of her nose!
    No, but with her nose that's quite a long way!

Why is your sister so thin?
    She never stops talking long enough to eat.

Smart Alec's sister wants to marry a man clever enough to make lots of money, and stupid enough to spend it all on her!

Kevin: 'What would I have to give you to get a kiss?'
Katie: 'An anaesthetic!'

What did the monster eat after he'd had all his teeth taken out?
    The dentist!

What does a monster do about flat feet?
    Uses a foot pump.

Jerry: 'Has your brother got a big mouth?'
Smart Alec: 'Big mouth? When he yawns you can't see his ears!'

Clair: 'Don't you think my shoes are becoming?'
Smart Alec: 'I'd say they were becoming rather worn out.'

Frightened passenger: 'How often does this sort of plane crash?'
Airline steward: 'Only once, sir.'

Why aren't monsters good dancers?
Because they've got three left feet.

What do you get if you try to take a ghost's photograph?
    Transparencies.

Sign in a delicatessen: Our tongue sandwiches speak for themselves!

Why's your dog called Ginger?
    Because Ginger snaps.

What does the Queen do when she belches?
    Issues a royal pardon.

How can you feed your brain?
    Eat noodle soup.

Mary: 'Say the three little words that will make me really happy.'
Mark: 'Push off home.'

Sam: 'My fiance is a man who is going places.'
Selina: 'The sooner the better, I'd say.'

Did you hear about the art-lover who lived on prunes? When he visited Paris, he spent all his time in the Louvre!

Anna: 'Has your mother-in-law got a pretty face?'
Donna: 'If you can read between the lines, yes.'

Ted: 'I hear your teacher's a worm.'
Fred: 'Yes, and he thinks everyone worships the ground he slithered out of!'

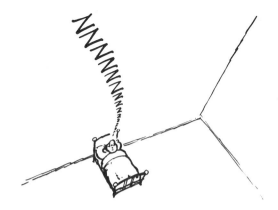

Teacher: 'Finish this proverb: Laugh and the world laughs with you...'
Smart Alec: 'Snore and you sleep alone'

Wayne: 'My sister's very temperamental.'
Dwayne: 'What do you mean?'
Wayne: 'She's half temper and half mental.'

Why are goldfish gold?
   So they don't go rusty.

Dad: 'When I was young my generation were called war babies.'
Smart Alec: 'I'm not surprised. I expect your parents took one look at you and started fighting.'

'I wouldn't say he was lazy, but the only exercise he gets is when he goes to see horror films. They make his flesh creep.'

Fred: 'Is your dad bald?'
Ted: 'Well he says he has flesh-coloured hair!'

Why did the bald man look out of the window?
    To get some fresh 'air.

Who wrote How to Survive Without Washing?
    I. Malone.

What's a ringleader?
    The first one in the bath.

Why did the secretary have the ends of her fingers chopped off?
    So she could write shorthand.

Why are skunks always fighting?
    Because they enjoy raising a stink.

Annie: 'Our neighbour is a great businesswoman.'
Danny: 'Does she run a shop?'
Annie: 'No, her nose is always in everyone else's business.'

Which airline do fleas fly on?
British Hairways.

Why did the cannibal join the police force?
So he could grill all his suspects.

JUST LET ME GET MY TEETH INTO THESE CRIMINALS!

Mrs. Smith: 'My husband has hundreds of men under him.'

Mrs. Jones: 'Oh really. Does he work in a cemetery?'

What's black, white, bruised and has eight wheels?

A novice nun on roller skates.

Mother: 'And what did your boss say when you told him you were leaving?'

Lucy: 'He said he was sorry I was leaving at the end of the month.'

Mother: 'He's probably sorry you're not leaving right away.'

What's a monster's favourite ballet?
    Swamp Lake.

Why didn't the shark eat the woman who fell off the ship?
    Because it was a man-eating shark!

What does a werewolf call a fur coat?
    Mummy.

How do you make a skeleton laugh?
    Tickle its funny bone.

Why did the cat cross the road?
    Because it was with the chicken.

Harry: 'I say Henry, that girl over there just rolled her eyes at me.'
Henry: 'Well roll them back, she might need them later.'

Sally and Susie were discussing their friend May. Sally said, 'Boys don't call her pretty, and they don't call her ugly. They just don't call her.'

Doctor: 'Good morning Mrs. Feather. I haven't seen you for a while.'
Mrs Feather: 'I know, doctor. That's because I've been ill.'

How do piranha fish win the football pools?
    With eight score jaws.

Why did the skunk take an aspirin?
    Because it had a stinking cold.

How does a ghost pass through a locked door?
    It uses a skeleton key.

*'Doctor, doctor, I think I've been bitten by
a vampire!'*
    'Drink this glass of water.'
'Will it make me better?'
    'No, but I'll be able to
see if your neck leaks.'

How did Dracula get into trouble?
    He over drew at the blood bank.

What did the vampire do when he retired?
    He buried himself in the country.

First ghost: 'Why are you so depressed?'
Second ghost: 'I don't seem to be able to frighten people anymore.'
First ghost: 'I know what you mean. We might as well be dead for all some people care.'

What do you call a collection of skunks?
    A phew!

What do you call two corpses in a church belfry?
  Dead ringers.

What kind of ghosts haunt hospitals?
  Surgical spirits.

What did Dracula write on his Christmas cards?
  Best vicious of the season.

Smart Alec: 'It would be better to die like Joan of Arc than like Charles I.'
History teacher: 'Why do you say that, Alec?'
Smart Alec: 'Well I reckon a grilled steak is better than a cold chop.'

Why do vampires never get fat?
    They eat necks to nothing.

*What does a headless
horseman ride?*
    A nightmare.

*What did the comedian say when someone
threw a turnip at him?*
    Would someone in the audience like
their head back?'

A criminal was sitting in the electric chair awaiting execution. As was the custom, he was asked by the jailers if he had any final requests.

'Yes,' he replied. 'Will you hold my hand?'

Knock! Knock!
Who's there?
Colleen.
Colleen who?
Colleen yourself up, you're absolutely filthy!

Lynn: 'Your sister should have lived in the Dark Ages.'
Flynn: 'Why's that?'
Lynn: 'She looks so awful in daylight.'

What do you get if you eat uranium?
    Atomic ache.

Waiter, waiter, there are two worms on my plate.
    Those are your sausages, sir.

What kind of jokes does a chiropodist like?
    Corny jokes.

Beth: 'Gulp! I've just swallowed a maggot.'
Ben: 'Shouldn't you take something for it?'
Beth: 'No, let it starve.'

David was standing at the top of an escalator looking at the handrail.

'Are you alright?' asked David's dad.

'Yes,' replied David. 'I'm just waiting for my chewing-gum to come round again.'

What has eight legs, four eyes and flies?
    Two cows in a plane.

What's blue and knocks on the window?
    An idiot in a goldfish bowl.

Mrs. Proudman: 'Samantha is so talented. She can do bird impressions, you know.'
Bored neighbour: 'Really? Does she sing?'
Mrs. Proudman: 'No, she eats worms.'

Doctor, doctor, my son's just swallowed some gunpowder.
    Well don't point him at me.

Doctor, doctor, Kenny keeps biting his nails!
    That's not serious in a child.
But Kenny bites his toenails!

Waiter, waiter, that curry has given me heartburn.
    What did you expect, sir, sunburn?

Waiter, waiter, there's a film on my soup.
    Oh dear, is it one you've seen before?

Cannibal in restaurant: 'I don't think much of your waiter.'
Manager: 'In that case, just eat the salad.'

What's large, smelly, covered in flies and lies upside-down in the gutter?
  A dead dustcart.

Why was Freddie called flatface?
Because he kept his nose to the grindstone.

How can you tell a professor of Ancient Greece?
  By his unwashed hair.

HAIRY
HONK!

Waiter, waiter, there's a dead fly in my soup.
Yes, sir, that's because they can't swim.

What did they call the clergyman who had a bright orange nose?
Belisha Deacon.

Who lived in the woods and stuck her tongue out at wolves?
Little Rude Riding Hood.

Waiter, the crust on my apple pie was tough.
That wasn't the crust, sir, it was the paper plate.

Waiter, waiter, what is that fly doing on my ice-cream?

I think it's learning how to ski, sir.

Susie: 'Mummy, Mummy, I just knocked over that ladder at the side of the house.'
Mum: 'Oh dear. I'd better go and tell Daddy.'
Susie: 'He already knows. He's hanging by his fingers from the bedroom windowsill!'

Soprano at concert: 'And what would you like me to sing next?'

Audience member: 'Do you know 'Old Man River'?'

Soprano: 'Er, yes.'

Audience member: 'Well, go and jump in it.'

Kenny: 'How did you get that black eye?'

Lenny: 'I was hit by some tomatoes.'

Kenny: 'But tomatoes are soft and squishy.'

Lenny: 'Not when they're in a tin, they're not.'

What's a frog's favourite drink?
  Croaka Cola.

Mrs. Houseproud: 'Wake up! There's a prowler downstairs. I think he's eating the leftovers from our dinner.'

Mr. Houseproud: 'In that case he won't last long. I'll phone the undertaker tomorrow.'

What happened to the burglar who fell in the concrete mixer?
He became a hardened criminal.

Why do traffic lights keep turning red?
    Well, what would you do if you kept having to stop and go in the middle of the road?

Who wears wool and lurex underwear?
    Long John Silver.

What does a modern undertaker call his funeral establishment?
    The departure lounge.

Why did the idiot keep his friend under the bed?
    Because he thought he was a little potty!

Knock! Knock!
    Who's there?
Euripedes.
    Euripedes who?
Euripedes you buy me a new pair.

Who herded phantom sheep?
    Little Boo Peep.

What time of the year is it when you sit on a pin?
  Spring.

Why did the monster give up boxing?
  He was afraid he'd spoil his looks.

Sam, Sam, the dirty man,
Washed his face in the frying-pan;
Combed his hair with a donkey's tail,
And scratched his back with his big toe-nail.

Which ghost made friends with the three bears?
    Ghouldilocks.

Knock! Knock!
    Who's there?
Alec.
    Alec who?
Alec Samantha but I don't like you.

How can you work out the cost of a funeral?
  By dead reckoning.

Who won the monster's beauty competition?
  No one.

What is engraved on a robot's tombstone?
  Rust in peace.

Dim Dennis: 'I went to see a mind reader last week.'
Donald: 'And what happened?'
Dim Dennis: 'He gave me my money back.'

Dave: 'I'd go to the ends of the earth for you.'
Debbie: 'What's stopping you?'

What did the sausage say as it was about to be put on a skewer?
Spear me, oh spear me!

Waiter, is there egg custard on the menu?
Not now, sir. I've wiped it off.

David: 'How's your brother getting on with his driving lessons?'
Smart Alec: 'I think he must have taken a crash course.'

Dim Dennis: 'My new shoes hurt.'
Mum: 'That's because you've got them on the wrong feet.'
Dim Dennis: 'But these are the only feet I've got!'

Film fan: 'You look familiar. Aren't you in films?'
Film star: 'On and off. How do you like me?'
Film fan: 'Off.'

What do you get if you cross a rabbit with a leek?
    A bunion.

What happened when the idiot had a brain transplant?
    The brain rejected him.

Why do bulldogs have flat faces?
    Because they chase too many parked cars!

Knock! Knock!
Who's there?
Jupiter.
Jupiter who?
Jupiter worm down my trousers?

What does a zombie do when he's had a shock?
Mixes a stiff drink.

How do you spot an idiot in a carwash?
He's the one on the bicycle.

What did the idiot hitch-hiker do?
Set off early to avoid the traffic.

Why was the robot hopping down the road making funny noises?

Because he had a screw loose.

Smart Alec: 'What's the difference between an ice-cream and a rat?'
Dim Dennis: 'I don't know.'
Smart Alec: 'Okay, I'll eat the ice-cream, you can eat the rat!'

Danny: 'My sister has a heart of gold.'
Smart Alec: 'It must match her teeth.'

What do you get if you cross a skeleton with a bag of crisps?

Snacks that go 'crunch!' in the night.

Ben: 'Will you help me blow up my bicycle tyres?'

Smart Alec: 'Certainly. Where's the gunpowder?'

Why did the cow jump over the moon?

Because the milkmaid's hands were cold.

Sarah Jane: 'My skin's all red from sitting in the sun too long.'

Smart Alec: 'You got what you basked for!'

What is a mushroom?
    A place where school dinners are cooked!

Mr. Jones: 'I got a new car for my wife yesterday.'
Mr. Davis: 'Wonderful! What do you think I'd get if I swapped mine?'

Why do witches have chemistry sets?
    To make magic smells.

YOU CAN REALLY GET YOUR TEETH INTO THESE JOKES.

Why did the idiot visit the dentist?
    To get a wisdom tooth.

How do you spot an idiot at an airport?
    He's the one throwing bread at the planes.

What's the difference between school dinners and tinned cat food?
    School dinners are served on plates and cat food is served on saucers.

Which nut invaded England?
　　William the Conker.

Doctor, doctor, what can you give me for wind?
　　How about a kite?

Harry goes to the dentist twice a year.
　　Really?
Yes, once for each tooth.

Why are dentists unhappy?
　　Because they spend all their time looking
down in the mouth.

Daisy: 'The problem is, I don't know what to do with my hands when I'm talking.'
Dolly: 'Why not hold them over your mouth?'

Doctor, doctor, I feel like a bucket.
    You look a bit pale.

Lynn: 'My boyfriend is so good looking, he's like an ancient Greek statue.'
Flynn: 'And like an ancient Greek statue, he's not all there.'

Waiter, waiter, this chop is very tough!
    It's a karate chop, sir!

Restaurant manager: 'Waiter! These tablecloths are filthy. They look as if they haven't been changed for a month!'
Waiter: 'Then it's not my fault, sir. I've only been here a week!'

Where do ghosts go on holiday?
    Wails.

Knock! Knock!
    Who's there?
Godfrey.
    Godfrey who?
Godfrey hairs sticking out of your nose!

Silly Selina: 'To get the ideal figure, I need to lose between ten and twenty pounds.'
Smart Alec: 'I'll take twenty pounds off you, then I can buy some new tyres for my bike.'

What did Silly Selina call her pet tiger?
Spot!
Mother: 'You're pretty dirty, Annie.'
Annie: 'I'm even prettier when I'm clean.'

What did the strawberry say to the maggot?
   You're boring me!

Doctor, doctor, my wife keeps putting me in the dustbin.
  Don't talk rubbish!

What did the zombie say when he knocked on Eddie's door?
  Eddie body home?

Why did the skeleton go on holiday?
  So he could get a skeletan.

Davis: 'You've got a ladder in your tights.'
Mavis: 'But I'm not wearing tights.'

Doctor, doctor, how do I stand?
    That's what's puzzling
me, Mrs. Jenkins.

My Auntie's gone on holiday to the West Indies.
    Jamaica?
No, she wanted to go.

First flea: 'You don't look too well.'
Second flea: 'I'm not really feeling up to scratch.'

What do you get if you cross a beetle with a mattress?
    A bed bug.

Why does a witch ride on a broom?
    Because a vacuum cleaner is too heavy to fly.

What do birds that lay square eggs say?
    Ouch!

Why was the angel rushed to hospital?
    Harp failure.

Who exploded at Waterloo?
    Napoleon Blownapart.

What kind of dogs do hairdressers have?
   Shampoodles.

Mike: 'A dog bit my ankle yesterday.'
Spike: 'Did you put anything on it?'
Mike: 'No, he seemed to like it just as it was.'

What fish tastes the best with cream?
    A jellyfish.

Milly: 'That's my school hat you're wearing.'
Molly: 'No, it isn't. Yours is the one I dropped in the river.'

Sam: 'I'll cook you a meal tomorrow. What would you like?'
Simon: 'I'd like to take out life insurance.'

What kind of dogs have the most ticks?
    Watch dogs.

Why are babies so happy?
   Because it's such a nappy time!

Smart Alec: 'I was at the zoo on Saturday.'
Steve: 'So was I!'
Smart Alec: 'Funny, I didn't see you in any of the cages.'

Alan: 'There were a lot of fans at the football match.'
Smart Alec: 'So that's why it was so cold!'

Why wouldn't the piglets listen to their dad?
   They thought he was such an old boar.

What do you call a cat's flat?
    A scratch pad.

Milly: 'You can't sleep in that room. What about the cockroaches?'
Billy: 'They'll just have to get used to me.'

What do you call a stupid monster?
    A dummy mummy.

Judge: 'Do you plead guilty or not guilty?'
Man in dock: 'Is there a third choice?'

How do you make mice smell nice?
    Use a mousewash.

What has three tails, twelve legs, and can't see?
    Three blind mice.

What should you do if you see a green monster at the end of the garden?
    Wait until it ripens.

What kind of meat did Dracula refuse to eat?
  Steak.

Why didn't the skeleton enjoy his job?
  Because his heart just wasn't in it.

How would a skunk smell if it didn't have a nose?
  Just as awful!

What did one ghost say to the other?
  I'm afraid I just don't believe in people.

What's a vampire's favourite soup?
    Scream of chicken.

Doctor, doctor, I can't get to sleep at night.
    Lie on the edge of the bed and you'll soon
drop off!

*Doctor, doctor, I'm putting on weight in certain
places. What should I do?*
    Stay out of those places.

Why can't a ghost tell a lie?
　　Because you can see right through it!

Joe: 'I never kissed my wife before we were married. Did you?'
James: 'I don't know. What was her name before she was married?'

Arthur: 'Our dog is like one of the family.'
Smart Alec: 'Really? Who?'

Ted: 'Ben is a very economical boy, isn't he?'
Ned: 'Well, he certainly saves on soap and water.'

Sheila: 'I've just got engaged, look at my lovely ring!'

Sarah: 'Is your fiance tall, handsome, blue-eyed with a scar on his left cheek?'

Sheila: 'How could you tell all that just by looking at the ring?'

Sarah: 'Easily. I gave that back to him last year.'

Jane: 'Is it true you only married Jonathan for the money his grandad left him?'

Janice: 'Certainly not. I would have married him no matter who had left him the money.'

Nurse: 'Are your teeth all your own, Mr. Fang?'

Mr. Fang: 'Whose do you think they are?'

What do you get if you cross a snowman with a werewolf?

Frostbite.

Darren: 'How old's your dad?'
Dave: 'I don't know. There were so many candles on his last birthday cake we had to call the Fire Brigade.'

Can you catch dandruff?

Only if you brush your hair over a carrier bag!

What lies in a cot and wobbles?

A jelly baby.

Knock! Knock!
   Who's there?
Juliet.
   Juliet who?
Juliet too much and
now she feels sick.

What's the best cure for seasickness?
   Bolting down your food.

Why did Dracula eat strong mints?
   Because he had bat breath.

Casualty nurse: 'Have an accident?'
Patient: 'No, thanks, I've just had one.'

What do you call a sleuthing skeleton?
  Sherlock Bones.

What do you get if you drop a piano down a mine shaft?
  A flat miner.

What did the ghost teacher say?
  'Watch the board children, and I'll go through it again!'

What does a ghost teacher get when she retires?
   A ghould watch.

What did Emma Hamilton say to Lord Nelson?
   You're the one eye love.

Mummy, Mummy, what's a werewolf?
   Stop asking questions and go and comb your face.

Doctor: 'May I take your pulse?'
Ms. Merry: 'Haven't you got one of your own?'

Johnny: 'All the boys at school call me bighead.'
Dad: 'Don't worry son, there's nothing in it.'

What do you call a small vampire?
  A pain in the knee!

*Why did the cannibal feel sick
after eating the missionary?*
  Because you can't keep
a good man down.

Why did the sword swallower leave the circus?
His ringmaster wanted him to take a cut.

What do you get if you cross a goat with a pig?
A dirty kid.

Teacher: 'To what family does the hippopotamus belong?'
Molly: 'I don't know, but it's no one in our road.'

What did the werewolf say to its victim?
So long, its been nice to gnaw you.